T0068031

HELL FIRE
NOT A
LITERAL FIRE

EMMANUEL KWADWO ADARKWAH

Order this book online at www.trafford.com
or email orders@trafford.com

Most Trafford titles are also available at major online book retailers.

All scripture quotations are taken from the New King James Version of the Holy Bible.

Printed in the United States of America.

ISBN: 978-1-4669-0203-9 (sc)
ISBN: 978-1-4669-0219-0 (e)

Trafford rev. 11/01/2011

North America & International
toll-free: 1 888 232 4444 (USA & Canada)
phone: 250 383 6864 • fax: 812 355 4082

CONTENTS

Chapter 1

INTRODUCTION

The issue of whether hell exist or not and the location of hell has never crossed my mind because I was made to believe from childhood that there is a place called hell beneath the earth where souls of sinners will be after the first death.

"[27]And as it is appointed for men to die once, but after this the judgment," (Hebrews 9:27)

Probably, if I had thought about it, I would have asked the same questions as being asked by many people who wants to find out the truth about hell. Our Lord Jesus Christ said,

"[32]And you shall know the truth and the truth shall make you free." (John 8:32)

Does Hell really exist?

Where is Hell?

What is the location of Hell?

Are the souls of sinners going to be burnt with literal fire?

These are but a few questions bothering the minds of lot of believers who wish to know the truth about hell and hell fire.

Hell and hell fire are topics in the Bible, which many believers have misconstrued. There is no doubt in the minds of Christians hell exist, so I will not delve into that.

This is because the Lord Jesus Christ whom we follow confirmed the reality of hell and made mention of it several times in the Bible.

However, we have been made to believe that there is a geographical place called hell where sinners will find themselves after death and they will be tormented day and night with an unquenchable literal fire.

Those with this believe argue that hell is in the crust of the earth by backing their argument with **Matthew 12:40** and **Ephesians 4:9.**

Jesus Christ said,

"For as Jonas was three days and three nights in the whale's belly: so shall the Son of man

be three days and three nights in the HEART OF THE EARTH." (Matthew 12:40)

Paul in his message to the Ephesians also said,

"Now that he ascended, what is it but that he also descended first into the LOWER PARTS OF THE EARTH." (Ephesians 4:9)

In addition, those of the view that souls of sinners are going to be tormented in hell with literal fire also quote the following scriptures to back their viewpoint.

"[42]And will cast them into the FURNACE OF FIRE. There will be wailing and gnashing of teeth." (Matthew 13:42)

"[41]Depart from Me, you cursed, into the EVERLASTING FIRE prepared for the devil and his angels :" (Matthew 25:41)

"[43]If your hand causes you to sin, cut it off. It is better for you to enter into life maimed, rather than having two hands, TO GO TO HELL, INTO THE FIRE THAT SHALL NEVER BE QUENCHED—[44]where 'THEIR WORM DOES NOT DIE AND THE FIRE IS NOT QUENCHED.'[45] And if your foot causes you to sin, cut it off. It is better for you to enter life lame, rather than having two feet, TO BE CAST INTO HELL, INTO THE FIRE THAT SHALL NEVER BE QUENCHED—[46]WHERE 'THEIR WORM DOES NOT DIE AND THE FIRE IS NOT QUENCHED.'

[47]And if your eye causes you to sin, pluck it out. It is better for you to enter the kingdom of God with one eye, rather than having two eyes, TO BE CAST INTO HELL FIRE— [48]WHERE 'THEIR WORM DOES NOT DIE AND THE FIRE IS NOT QUENCHED.'" (Mark 9:43-48)

"[24]Then he cried and said, 'Father Abraham, have mercy on me, and send Lazarus that he may dip the tip of his finger in water and cool my tongue; FOR I AM TORMENTED IN THIS FLAME.'" (Luke 16:24)

"[15]And anyone not found written in the Book of Life was cast into the LAKE OF FIRE." (Revelation 20:15)

Even if you have not read the above quoted scriptures before, after going through them, what is your say on the description of hell?

Are these descriptions of hell metaphorical or exactly as a layman understands?

Are they exactly what we have been made to believe all these years we came to know Christ?

Is there a place called hell?

Are sinners truly going to be tormented day and night with a literal fire forever?

The questions go on.

According to Bible theologians, the word "hell" is used 54 times in the old King James Version of the Bible and it is translated from several different words with various meaning.

It appears 31 times in the Old Testament from the Hebrew word "Sheol" meaning "the grave"

In the New Testament, 10 times from the Greek word "Hades" meaning "the grave",12 times from the Greek word "Gehenna" meaning "a place of burning" and once from the the Greek word "Tartarus" meaning "a place of darkness"

However, whether these words used to describe hell are really, what hell is or they were used figuratively will gradually be unfolded by the Lord to His chosen vessels as the Bible tells us knowledge will abound in the last days.

"[4] But you, Daniel, shut up the words, and seal the book until the time of the end; many shall run to and fro, and knowledge shall increase." (Daniel 12:4)

Chapter 2

GOD HAS NOT GIVEN US A SPIRIT OF FEAR

There are many stories of people who say they have been to hell and back or have had visions of hell. According to most of them, they claim they saw souls burning in literal fire. Some also claim they saw ugly creatures who were torturing the souls who ended up in a place called hell. You may have read or heard such stories that might or might not have had impact on your life. Among such people who said they have been to hell and back is Bill Wiese.

In Bill Wiese testimony of being in hell for 23 minutes, he said "In Job 7:14 it says, ***"THOU SCAREST ME WITH DREAMS AND TERRIFIETH ME WITH VISIONS."*** So this is definitely what the Lord did, terrified me through a vision. Also in returning from this, it took me a year to calm down, and become like a normal person again. I was so upset and traumatized from the fear that it's changed my whole viewpoint on how to witness and how much to appreciate what God saved us from." (Bill Wiese, 23 Minutes in Hell. Retrieved from http://spiritlessons.com/documents/billwiese_23minutesinhell_text.htm July 23, 2011).

"[14] Then You scare me with dreams And terrify me with visions," (Job 7:14)

Job made this statement because as human as he was, he thought God had brought those calamities on him not knowing the devil was doing that to him.

The devil was scaring Job with dreams and terrifying him with visions but not God. The aim of the devil for doing this to Job was for Job to denounce and curse the God he served.

The proceeding scriptures tell us that it was not God who inflicted the pain on Job but it was the devil because he, the devil wanted Job to curse and forsake God and that has been his trick since he fell from his position. He wants man to see God as wicked and not the loving and merciful God. His aim is for man to forsake God.

"[6] Now there was a day when the sons of God came to present themselves before the LORD, and Satan also came among them. [7] And the LORD said to Satan, "From where do you come?" So Satan answered the LORD and said, "From going

to and fro on the earth, and from walking back and forth on it." [8] Then the LORD said to Satan, "Have you considered My servant Job, that *there is* none like him on the earth, a blameless and upright man, one who fears God and shuns evil?" [9] So Satan answered the LORD and said, "Does Job fear God for nothing? [10] Have You not made a hedge around him, around his household, and around all that he has on every side? You have blessed the work of his hands, and his possessions have increased in the land. [11] BUT NOW, STRETCH OUT YOUR HAND AND TOUCH ALL THAT HE HAS, AND HE WILL SURELY CURSE YOU TO YOUR FACE!" [12] AND THE LORD SAID TO SATAN, "BEHOLD, ALL THAT HE HAS *IS* IN YOUR POWER; ONLY DO NOT LAY A HAND ON HIS *PERSON*." So, Satan went out from the presence of the LORD." (Job 1:6-12)

The devil is doing this to make people to see God as a wicked God and begin to curse Him by tormenting them with dreams of being in a place called hell burning with fire and terrifying them with visions of ugly creatures.

After the devil had done all these things to Job but still job did not denounce his God, he went back to God to ask for his health.

"[1]Again there was a day when the sons of God came to present themselves before the LORD, and Satan came also among them to present

himself before the LORD. [2] And the LORD said to Satan, "From where do you come?" Satan answered the LORD and said, "From going to and fro on the earth, and from walking back and forth on it." [3] Then the LORD said to Satan, "Have you considered My servant Job, that *there is* none like him on the earth, a blameless and upright man, one who fears God and shuns evil? And still he holds fast to his integrity, although you incited Me against him, to destroy him without cause." [4] So Satan answered the LORD and said, "Skin for skin! Yes, all that a man has he will give for his life. [5] BUT STRETCH OUT YOUR HAND NOW, AND TOUCH HIS BONE AND HIS FLESH, AND HE WILL SURELY CURSE YOU TO YOUR FACE!" [6] AND THE LORD SAID TO SATAN, "BEHOLD, HE *IS* IN YOUR HAND, BUT SPARE HIS LIFE." [7] SO SATAN WENT OUT FROM THE PRESENCE OF THE LORD, AND STRUCK JOB WITH PAINFUL BOILS FROM THE SOLE OF HIS FOOT TO THE CROWN OF HIS HEAD." (Job 2:1-7)

Bill Wiese in his testimony also said," One Demon just grabbed me and picked me up, and threw me into the wall like a glass. He just picked me up like a glass. That was how light I was, or how strong he was. And threw me into the wall, and every bone in my body just broke. And I felt pain! I just began to lie on the floor there, crying out for mercy, but these creatures don't have any mercy at all, absolutely no mercy.

The one picked me up, and the other one, with his razor-sharp claws; he just shredded my flesh right off. He just tore it off, and had absolutely no care what so ever for this body that God so wonderfully made.

It had a hatred that was so intense against me. I wondered, "Why am I alive, why am I living through this? I don't understand why am I not dead." My flesh just hung there in ribbons. And there was no blood, just flesh hanging, because life is in the blood, and there is no life in Hell. And there is no water in Hell.

Then one of the demons grabbed me, and drug me back into the cell and began all these torments again, which I really hate to talk about, because I don't like to have to re-live the torment. They began to crush my skull. One demon grabbed me and tried to crush my head. I was screaming and begging for mercy, but no mercy! About this time they each grabbed an arm and a leg and were about to tear off my legs and my arms. I thought, "I can't endure this, I can't endure this!"." (Bill Wiese, 23 Minutes in Hell. Retrieved from http://spiritlessons.com/documents/billwiese_23minutesinhell_text.htm July 23, 2011).

What the devil is doing is using these visions of physical torture in hell by literal fire and some ugly creatures to put fear in men for them to believe that God is a wicked God and not that loving God He says He is and by so doing begin to denounce Him as their God. However, the Bible makes us understand that He has not given us the spirit of fear.

"[15]For you did not receive the spirit of bondage again to fear, but you received the Spirit of adoption by whom we cry out, "Abba, Father."" (Romans 8:15)

"[7] For God has not given us a spirit of fear, but of power and of love and of a sound mind." (2 Timothy 1:7)

He, the devil, shows these people such images to terrify them and as they also spread these messages of their visions of hell, some people are turned to God out of fear whereas others begin to see God as a wicked God and for that matter, they will not serve Him. However, in Apostle Paul's letter to the Philippians, he said,

"[15] Some indeed preach Christ even from envy and strife, and some also from goodwill: [16] The former preach Christ from selfish ambition, not sincerely, supposing to add affliction to my chains; [17] but the latter out of love, knowing that I am appointed for the defence of the gospel.[18] What then? ONLY *THAT* IN EVERY WAY, WHETHER IN PRETENSE OR IN TRUTH, CHRIST

IS PREACHED; and in this I rejoice, yes, and will rejoice." (Philippians 1:15-18)

I am not saying the people who claim had been in hell or have had visions of hell are doing that for selfish ambitions, not at all. What I mean is the devil is using such images to put fear in men and for people to begin to see God in a different nature than the loving and merciful God we know.

However, while some are being turned away from God by these stories, others are being saved. The fact that some are being saved by those stories about hell, do not make hell and hell fire what those stories say they are.

It is not the nature of God to scare people in order to draw them to himself. Whenever God tells me to do something for him and I disobey, He chastens me but does not scare me.

"[5] And you have forgotten the exhortation which speaks to you as to sons: *"My son, do not despise the chastening of the LORD, Nor be discouraged when you are rebuked by Him;[6] For whom the LORD loves He chastens, And scourges every son whom He receives."*" (Hebrews 12:5-6)

Nonetheless, after a while, He comes around to console me as a mother sometimes consoles her ward after punishing him and gives me promises upon promises. He always shows His love to me. It is the work of the devil to put fear in us and not God. He does that when we disobey God because disobedience separates us from God and makes us lose our faith in God. He takes the advantage to accuse us, making us believe God will never forgive us.

"[10] **Then I heard a loud voice saying in heaven, "Now salvation, and strength, and the kingdom of our God, and the power of His Christ have come, FOR THE ACCUSER OF OUR BRETHREN, WHO ACCUSED THEM BEFORE OUR GOD DAY AND NIGHT, HAS BEEN CAST DOWN. "(Revelation 12:10)**

This reminds me of my first year at the University of Ghana when God began to speak audibly to me on something I had to do on campus, which I always gave an excuse to do later.

After two years of repeatedly hearing this message from God, "Emmanuel, pray." and immediately afterwards, another voice would also tell me to wait until I got to medical school before I started to pray, I stopped hearing this audible voice. I could no longer hear this voice because even though I do not remember praying to God to help me go to medical school, some way and some somehow within me, I became angry with God for not going to the medical school to the point where I began to despise hearing the word of God. The devil really enjoys when we become angry with God. This is because it gives him the opportunity to take advantage of our weaknesses when we become angry with God and move away from His presence.

What happened next?

In my third year, the devil put this fear in me that I was going to die immediately after completion of my undergraduate programme. I actually had this spirit of fear of death hunting me throughout the rest of my stay on campus. I will not go into details as to what the spirit of fear of death does, but it makes you lose your hope and aspirations in life. This continued until the Lord began to speak to me again after completion of my undergraduate course in 2006.

The devil put this fear in me. I could have said it was God because before then God had asked me to do a thing, which I did not do. Therefore, after sometime, the Lord stopped speaking to me and the devil took over and put that fear in me. It is not the nature of God to put fear in His disobedient or prodigal children.

"[15]**For you did not receive the spirit of bondage again to fear, but you received the**

Spirit of adoption by whom we cry out, "Abba, Father."" (Romans 8:15)

"7 For God has not given us a spirit of fear, but of power and of love and of a sound mind." (2 Timothy 1:7)

The devil tries to deceive us into believing that God does not love us by bringing images to us to portray the wickedness of God.

As he deceived Adam and Eve in the Garden of Eden, he is still in the same business of deception. He is really a cunning creature as written in the Bible,

"1 Now the serpent was more cunning than any beast of the field which the LORD God had made. And he said to the woman, "Has God indeed said, 'You shall not eat of every tree of the garden'?"" (Genesis 3:1)

That was not what God told Adam. God did not tell Adam not to eat every tree of the garden.

"16 And the LORD God commanded the man, saying, "Of every tree of the garden you may freely eat; 17 but of the tree of the knowledge of good and evil you shall not eat, for in the day that you eat of it you shall surely die."" (Genesis 2:16-17)

The same way the devil will not tell a believer Hell does not exist because the believer will realize it is the devil and rebuke him immediately. This is because the Lord Jesus Christ whom we follow made mention of it several times in the Bible.

The devil in his cunning way is telling believers hell really exists but he is using false images of hell to put fear in us and also sway some believers from believing that the God we serve is a loving and merciful God who has no delight in the sinner perishing.

"[23]Do I have any pleasure at all that the wicked should die?" says the Lord GOD, "*and* not that he should turn from his ways and live?" (Ezekiel 18:23)

"[32]For I have no pleasure in the death of one who dies," says the Lord GOD. "Therefore turn and live!" (Ezekiel 18:32)

His aim is to make people believe that God is a wicked God whose delight is in the suffering of the wicked but that is not the nature of God as the above stated scriptures shows. Do not forget that the devil is a liar and the father of it." **(John 8:44)**

Chapter 3

HELL: A STATE AND NOT A PLACE

Heaven and hell are not places that have geographical locations but they are states in which souls will find themselves after death. For we are made to understand that

"[27] And as it is appointed for men to die once, but after this the judgment," (Hebrews 9:27)

After the first death, the souls of men either ascend to heaven or descend into hell. Righteous souls will rise to heaven whereas unrighteous souls will descend into hell.

When our Lord Jesus Christ died on the cross after He was made sin for us (**2 Corinthians 5:21)**, He descended into hell.

"For as Jonas was three days and three nights in the whale's belly: so shall the Son of man be three days and three nights in the HEART OF THE EARTH." (Matthew 12:40)

"Now that he ascended, what is it but that he also descended first into the LOWER PARTS OF THE EARTH." (Ephesians 4:9)

The Richman and Lazarus

"[19]There was a certain rich man who was clothed in purple and fine linen and fared sumptuously every day. [20] But there was a certain beggar named Lazarus, full of sores, who was laid at his gate, [21] desiring to be fed with the crumbs which fell from the rich man's table. Moreover the dogs came and licked his sores. [22] So it was that the beggar died, and was carried by the angels to Abraham's bosom. The rich man also died and was buried. [23] And being in torments in Hades, he lifted up his eyes and saw Abraham afar off, and Lazarus in his bosom. [24] "Then he cried and said, 'Father Abraham, have mercy on me, and send Lazarus that he may dip the tip of his finger in water and cool my tongue; for I am tormented in this flame.' [25] But Abraham said, 'Son, remember that in your lifetime you received your good things, and likewise Lazarus evil things; but now he is comforted and you are tormented. [26] And besides all this, between us and you there is a great gulf fixed, so that those who want to pass from here to you cannot, nor can those from there pass to us.' [27] "Then he said, 'I beg you therefore, father, that you would send him to my father's house, [28] for I have five

brothers, that he may testify to them, lest they also come to this place of torment.' [29] Abraham said to him, 'They have Moses and the prophets; let them hear them.' [30] And he said, 'No, father Abraham; but if one goes to them from the dead, they will repent.' [31] But he said to him, 'If they do not hear Moses and the prophets, neither will they be persuaded though one rise from the dead." (Luke 16:19-31)

Let us examine the story of the Richman and Lazarus of whom the Lord Jesus Christ spoke about.

"[23] And being in torments in Hades, he lifted up his eyes and saw Abraham afar off, and Lazarus in his bosom." (v.23)

He lifted up his eyes because he, the rich man was in hell, which is a lower state than heaven, the state in which Abraham and Lazarus were.

Let me give this scenario. Someone in stage 4 does not look up to someone in stage 1 to help him solve his problems, but rather looks up to someone in stage 5 or 6. In the same line, someone who needs money does not go to someone who is poorer than he is for help, but rather goes to someone who is richer than he is, for he believes he is capable of helping him.

Heaven is a higher state than hell and therefore anyone in hell requiring help will have to lift up his eyes to heaven, where he believes help will come from.

The Psalmist said,

"[1]I will lift up my eyes to the hills—From whence comes my help?[2] My help *comes* from the LORD, Who made heaven and earth." (Psalm 121:1-2)

His help indeed comes from the Lord who is in heaven. The Lord Jesus Christ in His teaching on prayer taught us to begin our prayer in this manner.

"[9] . . . Our Father in heaven . . ." (Matthew 6:9)

This tells us that our spiritual Father, who is God, dwells in heaven and it is from only Him our help can come from.

The apostle Paul in his epistle to the Philippians said,

"[19] And my God shall supply all your need according to His riches in glory by Christ Jesus." (Philippians 4:19)

This need include protection, good health, shelter, food and all the things that come along with salvation.

Some people also believe hell is in the crust of the earth but that is not true. Such people read **Matthew 12:40** and **Ephesians 4:9** and take the words written there literally. As a believer, you need to ask the Spirit of God to open the eyes of your understanding to be able to understand the Word of God. There are so many hidden secrets in the Word of God, which gradually God is revealing to His children. We are made to understand in Daniel that knowledge shall increase in the last days **(Daniel 12:4).**

Ask for wisdom, knowledge, revelation and understanding and they shall be given to you.

"[5]If any of you lacks wisdom, let him ask of God, who gives to all liberally and without reproach, and it will be given to him." (James 1:5)

"[6]For the LORD gives wisdom; From His mouth *come* knowledge and understanding;" (Proverbs 2:6)

The Psalmist said,

"[34] Give me understanding, and I shall keep Your law; Indeed, I shall observe it with *my* whole heart. (Psalm 119:34)

"[6] Behold, You desire truth in the inward parts, And in the hidden *part* You will make me to know wisdom." (Psalm 51:6)

Hence, do not read the Bible with your own understanding, but allow the Spirit of God to direct you.

"[13] However, when He, the Spirit of truth, has come, He will guide you into all truth; for He will not speak on His own *authority,* but whatever He hears He will speak; and He will tell you things to come." (John 16:13)

"[26] But the Helper, the Holy Spirit, whom the Father will send in My name, He will teach you all things, and bring to your remembrance all things that I said to you." (John 14:26)

Yes. It is true that when Jesus Christ died His soul went into hell, because the Bible makes us understand he took on the sins of men. However it is not true that His soul was in the crust of the earth as some believe that is where hell is according to **Matthew 12:40** and **Ephesians 4:9.**

Jesus Christ said,

"For as Jonas was three days and three nights in the whale's belly: so shall the Son of man be three days and three nights in the HEART OF THE EARTH." **(Matthew 12:40)**

Paul talking about Jesus in his message to the Ephesians also said, ***"Now that he ascended,***

what is it but that he also descended first into the LOWER PARTS OF THE EARTH." (Ephesians 4:9)

The heart of the earth is the lowest part of the earth and therefore, the Lord Jesus Christ used it figuratively to illustrate hell, which is the lowest state the soul of man can be, knowing His soul was going to be in this state after His death on the cross since he took on the sins of men. As the Bible makes us understand, before He could bring man back to God, He had to put on the sins of man and descend into this lowest state and it is after coming out of this state that salvation was made available to man.

"[24]Then he cried and said, 'Father Abraham, have mercy on me, and send Lazarus that he may dip the tip of his finger in water and cool my tongue; for I am tormented in this flame." (v.24)

He wanted Lazarus to dip his finger in the living water to quench his thirst. Our Lord Jesus Christ is the only person that can give this living water. This is the living water, which the Lord Jesus gives to us when we come to accept Him as our Lord and saviour. It is the living water, which quenches the thirst of our souls for the word of God for eternity.

The Lord Jesus Christ said to the Samaritan woman,

"[13]Whoever drinks of this water will thirst again, [14] but whoever drinks of the water that I shall give him will never thirst. But the water that I shall give him will become in him a fountain of water springing up into everlasting life." (John 4:13-14)

He also said,

"[35]I am the bread of life. He who comes to Me shall never hunger, and he who believes in Me shall never thirst." (John 6:35)

"On the last day, that great day of the feast, Jesus stood and cried out, saying, "If anyone thirsts, let him come to Me and drink. [38] He who believes in Me, as the Scripture has said, out of his heart will flow rivers of living water."" (John 7:37-38)

Those who will find themselves in the presence of God will continue to draw the living water that flows from the presence of God as written in **Revelation 22:1, Zechariah 14:8-9** and **Isaiah 12:1-3**;

"[1] And he showed me a pure river of water of life, clear as crystal, proceeding from the throne of God and of the Lamb. "(Revelation 22:1)

"[8]And in that day it shall be *That* living waters shall flow from Jerusalem, Half of them toward the eastern sea And half of them toward the western sea; In both summer and winter it shall occur. [9]And the LORD shall be King over all the earth. In that day it shall be—"The LORD *is* one," And His name one." (Zechariah 14:8-9)

"[1]And in that day you will say:" O LORD, I will praise You; Though You were angry with me, Your anger is turned away, and You comfort me.[2]Behold, God is my salvation, I will trust and not be afraid; 'For YAH, the LORD, is my strength and song; He also has become my salvation.'"[3]Therefore with joy you will draw water From the wells of salvation. (Isaiah 12:1-3)

However, the souls of those who rejected him and hence did not have the thirst of their souls for the word of God quenched while living on this earth will find themselves in a state burning for the Word, who is no longer available to them because they have been cut off from the presence of God.

That is what the rich man meant by ' . . . **FOR I AM TORMENTED IN THIS FLAME.**' He was burning for the word of God, whom he cannot have.

Their thirst will never be quenched because they have been cast out from the presence of

God, where the living water flows. Forever, they cannot come into the presence of God.

They will desire for the Word of God, whom they will not have.

They will yearn for the Word of God, whom they will not have.

They will burn for the Word of God, whom they will not have.

They will thirst for the Word of God, whom they will not have.

"[11] And I say to you that many will come from east and west, and sit down with Abraham, Isaac, and Jacob in the kingdom of heaven. [12] But the sons of the kingdom will be cast out into outer darkness. There will be weeping and gnashing of teeth." (Matthew 8:11-12)

They will be cast out into outer darkness, far from the presence of God, where there will be no light. This is because the Word of God, who is the light, will no longer be available to them.

"[1]In the beginning was the Word, and the Word was with God, and the Word was God. [2] He was in the beginning with God. [3] All things were made through Him, and without Him nothing was made that was made. [4] In Him was life, and the

life was the light of men. [5] And the light shines in the darkness, and the darkness did not comprehend it." (John 1:1-5)

These souls will be weeping for they will be in pain, anger and frustrated for not accepting the Lord Jesus Christ while they had the opportunity to do so. For they will forever be separated from God. Their thirst for the living water will forever not be quenched.

Chapter 4

FIRE: AS USED BY OUR LORD JESUS CHRIST

Many believers have been made to believe that the souls of unbelievers are going to be burnt with literal fire in a place called hell after the first death. This is far from the truth. I used to believe this till the Lord gave me this revelation.

Fire, as used by the Lord Jesus Christ to describe hell in the scriptures **(Matt 5:22; 7:19; 13:40,42,50; 18:8,9; 25:41, 25:41 Mark 9:47, Mark 9:43,44, 45,47,48)** means desire, yearn, burn, thirst, crave, long for and not really a literal fire.

"22 But I say to you that whoever is angry with his brother without a cause shall be in danger of the judgment. And whoever says to his brother, 'Raca!' shall be in danger of the council. But whoever says, 'You fool!' shall be in danger of HELL FIRE. (Matthew 5:22)

"[19] Every tree that does not bear good fruit is cut down and thrown into the FIRE." (Matthew 7:19)

"[40] Therefore as the tares are gathered AND BURNED IN THE FIRE, so it will be at the end of this age." (Matthew 13:40)

"[42] And will cast them into the FURNACE OF FIRE. There will be wailing and gnashing of teeth." (Matthew 13:42)

"[50] And cast them into the FURNACE OF FIRE. There will be wailing and gnashing of teeth." (Matthew 13:50)

"[8] If your hand or foot causes you to sin, cut it off and cast *it* from you. It is better for you to enter into life lame or maimed, rather than having two hands or two feet, to be cast into the EVERLASTING FIRE." (Matthew 18:8)

"[9] And if your eye causes you to sin, pluck it out and cast *it* from you. It is better for you to enter into life with one eye, rather than having two eyes, to be cast into HELL FIRE." (Matthew 18:9)

"[41] Then He will also say to those on the left hand, 'Depart from Me, you cursed, into the EVERLASTING FIRE prepared for the devil and his angels:" (Matthew 25:41)

Forever, they will desire for the Word of God, whom they will not have.

Forever, they will yearn for the Word of God, whom they will not have.

They will burn for the Word of God, whom they will not have for eternity.

They will thirst for the Word of God, whom they will not have eternally.

They will crave for the Word of God for everlasting, whom they will not have.

They will long for the Word of God forever, whom they will not have.

"[24]Then he cried and said, 'Father Abraham, have mercy on me, and send Lazarus that he may dip the tip of his finger in water and cool my tongue; for I am tormented in this flame." (v.24)

"[43]If your hand causes you to sin, cut it off. It is better for you to enter into life maimed, rather than having two hands, TO GO TO HELL, INTO THE FIRE THAT SHALL NEVER BE QUENCHED—[44]where 'THEIR WORM DOES NOT DIE AND THE FIRE IS NOT QUENCHED.'[45] And if your foot causes you to sin, cut it off. It is better for you to enter life lame, rather than having two feet, TO BE CAST INTO HELL, INTO

THE FIRE THAT SHALL NEVER BE QUENCHED—[46]WHERE 'THEIR WORM DOES NOT DIE AND THE FIRE IS NOT QUENCHED.' [47] And if your eye causes you to sin, pluck it out. It is better for you to enter the kingdom of God with one eye, rather than having two eyes, TO BE CAST INTO HELL FIRE— [48]WHERE 'THEIR WORM DOES NOT DIE AND THE FIRE IS NOT QUENCHED.'" (Mark 9:43-48)

When the Lord Jesus Christ says, '· · · · to be cast into hell fire—where *Their worm does not die And the fire is not quenched.', He simply means* the souls of those who will be found in hell will never be annihilated; neither the thirst of their souls for the Word of God will ever be quenched. They will live in everlasting damnation; thirsty for the Word of God.

"[11] And the smoke of their torment ascends forever and ever; and they have no rest day or night, who worship the beast and his image, and whoever receives the mark of his name." (Revelation 14:11)

According to **Revelation 14:11** their cry and plead for mercy will forever ascend to God, but He will have no mercy on them in the same way the plea of the rich man was not heeded to.

"[1]Behold, the LORD's hand is not shortened, That it cannot save; Nor His ear heavy,

That it cannot hear.[2] But your iniquities have separated you from your God; And your sins have hidden *His* face from you, So that He will not hear." (Isaiah 59:1-2)

As he did not spare the people of Sodom and Gomorrah, the same way these souls will never be spared.

"[4] For if God did not spare the angels who sinned, but cast *them* down to hell and delivered *them* into chains of darkness, to be reserved for judgment;[5] and did not spare the ancient world, but saved Noah, *one of* eight *people,* a preacher of righteousness, bringing in the flood on the world of the ungodly; [6] and turning the cities of Sodom and Gomorrah into ashes, condemned *them* to destruction, making *them* an example to those who afterward would live ungodly; [7]and delivered righteous Lot, *who was* oppressed by the filthy conduct of the wicked" (2 Peter 2:4-7)

They will forever be restless because their thirst for God will never be quenched.

Chapter 5

HELL FIRE IS NOT A LITERAL FIRE

I was at All-Night service at Baden Powell on 19th February 2011, when I had this revelation from the Lord. It came as a word of Knowledge.

"Hell fire is not a literal fire as some people think, but it is the state where souls will yearn for the word of God and will not have him. Their souls will be burning for the word of God, whom they cannot have. They will thirst for the living water, which is no longer available to them. They had the opportunity to drink from the fountain of life flowing with the living water, but they did not make use of that opportunity. Their souls will be restless and uncomfortable for eternity. Souls who do not accept the Lord Jesus Christ who came to die for the sins of mankind in order to bring us back to the Father will be burning for the word of God, thirsty for the living water, but it will be too late because they have been cut off from the presence of God forever."

The Spirit of God immediately drew my mind back to an experience I had around September and October 2009 after giving me this revelation and He told me that was how hell would be like. I understood him perfectly. This is something, which cannot easily be explained with words.

After several years of disobedience to the call of God, even though I yearn to be in His presence all the time, the Lord began to give me this warning. While in my room, a quiet place or sometimes, even in a vehicle, the Lord would come around and ask me a question, which I did not respond. He gave me the same message after asking this question.

He would ask, "Do you remember my servant Jonah?"

Then He will continue, "During his time, I used the whale, your time I will use my Spirit."

After about a year or two and several months giving me the same message and I was still disobedient to the call and warnings of God, the Spirit of God indeed took me to hell and that was when my soul was very much disturbed and uncomfortable.

For over a month, I could not feel happiness in my soul. My soul was restless throughout this period. Although, sometimes my soul felt sad when God told me to do something and I did not do it, but this was totally a different experience from what I used to know.

I wept when I was in office, vehicles and most of the time when I was alone. It is difficult to explain with words what I really went through. I tried to look for a place to hide from the Lord but nowhere to run to or hide, little did I know my soul was in hell.

"[15]And the kings of the earth, the great men, the rich men, the commanders, the mighty men, every slave and every free man, hid themselves in the caves and in the rocks of the mountains, [16] and said to the mountains and rocks, "Fall on us and hide us from the face of Him who sits on the throne and from the wrath of the Lamb! [17] For the great day of His wrath has come, and who is able to stand?" "(Revelation 6:15-17)

"[29] For indeed the days are coming in which they will say, 'Blessed *are* the barren, wombs that never bore, and breasts which never nursed!' [30] Then they will begin *'to say to the mountains, "Fall on us!" and to the hills, "Cover us!"*'"(Luke 23:29-30)

It got to a point where I told Him to kill me because I was tired, after all He could do whatever He wished to do. However, He did not respond to my plea for death to come upon me.

"[6]In those days men will seek death and will not find it; they will desire to die, and death will flee from them." (Revelation 9:6)

Therefore, immediately the Spirit of God reminded me of this experience and told me that was how hell would be like, I perfectly understood Him.

Although, it is not going to be a torment by literal fire as we have been made to believe all these years, it is not something I would wish any person to experience for eternity. Physical torture can never be compared to this.

Even though our Lord Jesus Christ was despised and rejected by men, chastised, stricken, smitten, wounded, bruised and afflicted, He was not heard complaining about any of the torture that was given to Him.

"[3]He is despised and rejected by men, A Man of sorrows and acquainted with grief. And we hid, as it were, *our* faces from Him; He was despised, and we did not esteem Him. [4] Surely He has borne our griefs And carried our sorrows; Yet we esteemed Him stricken, Smitten by God, and afflicted.[5] But He *was*

wounded for our transgressions, *He was* bruised for our iniquities; The chastisement for our peace *was* upon Him, And by His stripes we are healed." (Isaiah 53:3-5)

The real pain, anguish and suffering came when the Father turned His back on Him after taking on the sins of men.

"[24] Who Himself bore our sins in His own body on the tree, that we, having died to sins, might live for righteousness—by whose stripes you were healed." (1 Peter 2:24)

He cried out when He was cut off from the presence of the Father. His torment began when there was a separation of him, the Son from the Father.

"[46] And about the ninth hour Jesus cried out with a loud voice, saying, "Eli, Eli, lama sabachthani?" that is, *"My God, My God, why have You forsaken Me?"* (Matthew 27:46)

As you can fathom, the knowledge of separation from the Father was more painful to our Lord Jesus Christ than the physical torture he went through. My experience in hell also tells me the torment of being separated from the Father cannot be compared to any physical torment any person can imagine of.

When our Lord Jesus Christ got to know that the cities in which he did mighty works did not repent, He said to them,

"[21]"Woe to you, Chorazin! Woe to you, Bethsaida! For if the mighty works which were done in you had been done in Tyre and Sidon, they would have repented long ago in sackcloth and ashes. [22] But I say to you, it will be more tolerable for Tyre and Sidon in the day of judgment than for you. [23] And you, Capernaum, who are exalted to heaven, will be brought down to Hades; for if the mighty works which were done in you had been done in Sodom, it would have remained until this day. [24] But I say to you that it shall be more tolerable for the land of Sodom in the day of judgment than for you."" (Matthew 11:21-24)

Sodom and Gomorrah were destroyed by literal fire rained upon them.

"[24] Then the LORD rained down burning sulfur on Sodom and Gomorrah—from the LORD out of the heavens. [25] Thus he overthrew those cities and the entire plain, destroying all those living in the cities—and also the vegetation in the land. [26] But Lot's wife looked back, and she became a pillar of salt. [27] Early the next morning Abraham got up and returned to the place where he had stood before the LORD. [28] He looked down toward Sodom and Gomorrah, toward all the land of the plain, and he saw

dense smoke rising from the land, like smoke from a furnace." (Genesis 19:24-38)

So, if our Lord Jesus in His rebuke says it will be more tolerable for the land of Sodom than for us, this should inform you that the pain and torment those who find themselves in hell will be more than that of a mere literal fire.

This revelation made me aware that hell is not a place and has no geographical location, but a state, souls of sinners will find themselves. Souls of those who do not accept the Lord Jesus Christ as their Lord and saviour will be in this state forever.

This was a state prepared for the devil and the fallen angels when they tried to usurp the authority of the Most High God. They fell from a higher state, which is heaven to a lower state, which is hell.

"[41]Then He will also say to those on the left hand, 'Depart from Me, you cursed, into the everlasting fire prepared for the devil and his angels:" (Matthew 25:41)

"[12]How you are fallen from heaven, O Lucifer, son of the morning! *How* you are cut down to the ground, You who weakened the nations![13] For you have said in your heart:' I will ascend into heaven, I will exalt my throne

above the stars of God; I will also sit on the mount of the congregation On the farthest sides of the north; [14] I will ascend above the heights of the clouds, I will be like the Most High.' [15] Yet you shall be brought down to Sheol, To the lowest depths of the Pit." (Isaiah 14:12-15)

In an interview with *Time* Magazine November 15, 1993 edition (Vol. 142 No. 20) articled, "Of Angels, Devils and Messages From God", Billy Graham, a world renowned evangelist said this about hell:

"The only thing I could say for sure is that **HELL MEANS SEPARATION FROM GOD. WE ARE SEPARATED FROM HIS LIGHT, FROM HIS FELLOWSHIP. THAT IS GOING TO BE HELL. WHEN IT COMES TO A LITERAL FIRE, I DON'T PREACH IT BECAUSE I'M NOT SURE ABOUT IT. WHEN THE SCRIPTURE USES FIRE CONCERNING HELL THAT IS POSSIBLY AN ILLUSTRATION OF HOW TERRIBLE IT'S GOING TO BE—NOT FIRE BUT SOMETHING WORSE, A THIRST FOR GOD THAT CANNOT BE QUENCHED."**

Moreover, in his book, *Storm Warning*, he states, **"JESUS USED THIS SYMBOL [FIRE] OVER AND OVER. I BELIEVE THAT IT MEANS A THIRST FOR GOD THAT IS NEVER QUENCHED." (P. 263)**

John Paul II, the recent past pope of the Catholic Church, in a statement made on July 28, 1999 said,

"In a theological sense however, hell is something else: it is the ultimate consequence of sin itself, which turns against the person who committed it. It is the state of those who definitively reject the Father's mercy, even at the last moment of their life. The images of hell that Sacred Scripture presents to us must be correctly interpreted. They show the complete frustration and emptiness of life without God. **RATHER THAN A PLACE, HELL INDICATES THE STATE OF THOSE WHO FREELY AND DEFINITIVELY SEPARATE THEMSELVES FROM GOD, THE SOURCE OF ALL LIFE AND JOY.** This is how the *Catechism of the Catholic Church* summarizes the truths of faith on this subject: **"TO DIE IN MORTAL SIN WITHOUT REPENTING AND ACCEPTING GOD'S MERCIFUL LOVE MEANS REMAINING SEPARATED FROM HIM FOR EVER BY OUR OWN FREE CHOICE. THIS STATE OF DEFINITIVE SELF-EXCLUSION FROM COMMUNION WITH GOD AND THE BLESSED IS CALLED 'HELL'"** (n. 1033)." (John Paul II, General Audience, July 28, 1999. Retrieved from http://www.vatican.va/holy_father/john_paul_ii/audiences/1999/documents/hf_jp-ii_aud_28071999_en.html July 10, 2011).

N.T. Wright, a former Bishop of Durham of the Church of England in an interview on 100 Huntley Street (HD) 12th December 2008, also attested to the fact that hell is really a state of being and not a place.

"Hell is, if you like, I was going to say it's where God isn't. Even that isn't true, cause ultimately God will be all in all. But it is as though within Gods all in all-ness, there will be an absence, a loss, the possibility of there being creatures who were once human, but now are not. I don't know what the word where would mean at that point. Cause, I don't know what location is like at that point. And I fail to see why we should speculate about it. **I JUST THINK ITS A STATE OF BEING, OF CREATURES THAT ONCE WERE HUMAN, ONCE DID REFLECT THE IMAGE OF GOD, BUT HAVE CHOSEN TO DO SO NO MORE.** And I have to say, people often ask me about this, and I don't like talking about it, partly because I know a great many people and love a great many people, some of whom, as far as I can see are saying precisely that to God. And I shudder to think, of those people saying, I truly don't want to be human. Thank you very much . . . because they are lovely human beings at the moment, and you can see glimmers of God in them, but how that works out is up to them. So this is not something I talk about readily or happily. I know some Christians who, ah, there's heaven and there's hell. And those guys are going to get it. That's not what I'm saying at all. **THIS IS A MATTER OF REALLY A TERRIFYING POSSIBILITY.** And every so often you look in the mirror, and say, hmm. Are you worshipping idols as well. Is that where you're going. Christians have to ask themselves that. It doesn't destroy your assurance, but it's a question you need to ask." (http://www.100huntley.com/video.php?id=8Zk31Uc_pCY)

What does the scripture say? By the mouth of two or three witnesses every word may be established **(Matthew 18:16)**.

Chapter 6

JONAH IN HELL

The soul of Jonah was indeed found in hell for three days and three nights when he disobeyed God. He ended up in hell when he ran away from the presence of God.

"[1] Now the word of the LORD came to Jonah the son of Amittai, saying, [2] "Arise, go to Nineveh, that great city, and cry out against it; for their wickedness has come up before Me." [3] But Jonah arose to flee to Tarshish FROM THE PRESENCE OF THE LORD. He went down to Joppa, and found a ship going to Tarshish; so he paid the fare, and went down into it, to go with them to Tarshish FROM THE PRESENCE OF THE LORD.[10]Then the men were exceedingly afraid, and said to him, "Why have you done this?" For the men knew that he FLED FROM THE PRESENCE OF THE LORD, because he had told them." (Jonah 1:1-3,10)

He forgot the divine nature of God, as being Omniscient (all knowing), Omnipotent (all-powerful) and Omnipresent (present everywhere). Therefore, he tried to run away from His presence, even to the point of hiding himself in the lowest parts of the ship when he realized it was because of him that was why the calamity had come upon him and all those in the ship.

"[5]Then the mariners were afraid; and every man cried out to his god, and threw the cargo that *was* in the ship into the sea, to lighten the load. BUT JONAH HAD GONE DOWN INTO THE LOWEST PARTS OF THE SHIP, HAD LAIN DOWN, AND WAS FAST ASLEEP." (Jonah 1:5)

The Psalmist having this knowledge about God said,

"[7]Where can I go from Your Spirit? Or where can I flee from Your presence?[8] If I ascend into heaven, You *are* there;If I make my bed in hell, behold, You *are there." (*Psalm 139:7-8)

Jonah on the other hand, even though he was a prophet of God, lacked this knowledge and thought he could have run away from the presence of the Lord but rather ended up in hell.

"[4] Then I said, 'I have been cast out of Your sight; . . ." (Jonah 2:4)

His lack of knowledge in this respect led him to hell. For God said,

"[6] MY PEOPLE ARE DESTROYED FOR LACK OF KNOWLEDGE. Because you have rejected knowledge, I also will reject you from being priest for Me; Because you have forgotten the law of your God, I also will forget your children." (Hosea 4:6)

This is exactly what will happen to souls who reject the Lord Jesus Christ as their saviour.

They will be cut off from the presence of God. They will be separated from Him because of their disobedience. He will say to them,

"[41]Depart from Me, you cursed, into the EVERLASTING FIRE prepared for the devil and his angels :" (Matthew 25:41)

Although Jonah's body was in the belly of the whale, his soul was in hell. This was similar to the experience I had. Even though I was walking about like any other man, my soul was in hell.

"Do you remember my servant Jonah? During his time, I used the whale, your time I will use my Spirit."

However, even though we were (I mean Jonah and myself were disobedient to God, our hearts were still for God.

"[9] So he said to them, "I *am* a Hebrew; and I FEAR THE LORD, the God of heaven, who made the sea and the dry *land*."" (Jonah 1:9)

In his affliction, he cried out to the Lord as our Lord Jesus Christ cried out to our Father in heaven when He had forsaken Him while on the cross when he took on the sins of men.

Jonah said,**"[2]I cried out to the LORD because of my affliction, And He answered me. Out of the belly of Sheol I cried, And You heard my voice." (Jonah 2:2)**

However, while being afflicted in hell, Jonah prayed to the Lord for mercy and the Lord had mercy on him.

"[1]Then Jonah prayed to the LORD his God from the fish's belly.[2] And he said: "I cried out to the LORD because of my affliction, And He answered me." Out of the belly of Sheol I cried, And You heard my voice.[3] For You cast me into the deep, Into the heart of the seas, And the floods surrounded me; All Your billows and Your waves passed over me.[4] Then I said, 'I have been cast out of Your sight; Yet I will look again toward Your holy temple.' [5] The waters surrounded me, even to my soul; The deep closed around me; Weeds were wrapped around my head. [6] I went down to the moorings of the mountains; The earth with its bars closed behind me forever; Yet

You have brought up my life from the pit, O LORD, my God. [7] "When my soul fainted within me, I remembered the LORD; And my prayer went up to You, Into Your holy temple.[8] "Those who regard worthless idols Forsake their own Mercy. [9] But I will sacrifice to You With the voice of thanksgiving; I will pay what I have vowed. Salvation is of the LORD." [10] So the LORD spoke to the fish, and it vomited Jonah onto dry land. (Jonah 2)

The mercy of the Lord is available as long as you are alive. Walk in it and never depart from it.

"[15] For he says to Moses, I will have mercy on whom I have mercy, and I will have compassion on whom I have compassion." (Romans 9:15)

Nevertheless, God would not have mercy on those who disobeyed Him after judgment. Their cry and plead for mercy will forever ascend to Him, but He will have no mercy on them.

"[11] And the smoke of their torment ascends forever and ever; and they have no rest day or night, who worship the beast and his image, and whoever receives the mark of his name." (Revelation 14:11)

God will not hear their cry because their sins have closed His ears; neither will He see their torments because their iniquities have covered His face.

"[1]Behold, the LORD's hand is not shortened, That it cannot save; Nor His ear heavy, that it cannot hear.[2] But your iniquities have separated you from your God; And your sins have hidden *His* face from you, So that He will not hear." (Isaiah 59:1-2)

Jonah in his prayers to God acknowledges that only God can save man.

"[9]But I will sacrifice to You With the voice of thanksgiving; I will pay what I have vowed. SALVATION IS OF THE LORD." (Jonah 2:9)

Now is the day of salvation.

"[2]For He says:" *In an acceptable time I have heard you, And in the day of salvation I have helped you.*" Behold, now *is* the accepted time; behold, now *is* the day of salvation." (2 Corinthians 6:2)

Chapter 7

OUT OF BODY EXPERIENCE

On 6th August 2011 while sweeping my room, I began to think about this experience in hell. As I thought about it, the following questions ran through my mind;

"How can this be?

How could I still be alive and my soul was in hell?

Immediately, I was told by the Spirit of God that was an out of body experience. Then, I recalled what the Apostle Paul said in **2 Corinthians 12:2-4**,

"[2] I know a man in Christ who fourteen years ago—whether in the body I do not know, or whether out of the body I do not know, God knows—such a one was caught up to the third heaven. [3] And I know such a man—whether in the body or out of the body I do not know, God knows— [4]how he was caught up into Paradise

and heard inexpressible words, which it is not lawful for a man to utter."

He, Paul, was caught up into Paradise whereas I descended into hell. Although, I was alive and doing everything any living being could do, my soul was in hell.

First, I was in hell and I never knew that was hell only to be told by the Spirit of God over a year later after my experience that that was hell. Secondly, I had an out of body experience and I did not know either. I did not know because of not having experienced it before. I believe an out of body experience is an experience you will never know for the first time until the Spirit of God tells you.

I now understand Paul when he said,

". . . whether in the body I do not know, or whether out of the body I do not know, God knows . . ."

That was the first time Paul had this experience and was not sure whether he went to Paradise with his body or out of his body. He was not sure and that was the reason he said, ". . . God knows . . .". Yes. Only God who knows all the details of such experiences and His Spirit reveals to those whom He wishes to reveal. The Spirit of God knows the deep things of God and reveals them to us according to His will.

"[10] But God has revealed *them* to us through His Spirit. For the Spirit searches all things, yes, the deep things of God. [11] For what man knows the things of a man except the spirit of the man which is in him? Even so no one knows the things of God except the Spirit of God. [12] Now we have received, not the spirit of the world, but the Spirit who is from God, that we might know the things that have been freely given to us by God." (1 Corinthians 2:10-12)

My out of body experience as told me by the Spirit of God was a similar experience Jonah had. Although his body was in the belly of the whale, his soul was indeed in hell for three days and three nights.

"[1] Then Jonah prayed to the LORD his God from the fish's belly. [2] And he said:" I cried out to the LORD because of my affliction, And He answered me. "Out of the belly of Sheol I cried, *And* You heard my voice." "(Jonah 2:1-2)

Jonah indeed had an out of body experience for three days and three nights whereas mine was for over a month.

Nonetheless, we should be careful not to believe every out of body experience into Paradise or hell to be from God.

The Bible makes us understand that the devil always tries to portray himself as the angel of light and the reason for doing this is to deceive.

"[14] And no wonder! For Satan himself transforms himself into an angel of light." (2 Corinthians 11:14)

One of such out of body experience, which I believe was not from God, was the experience the prophet of God, Kenneth E. Hagin had at the age of 15. I have no doubt in my mind that Kenneth E. Hagin was a man of God whom God used mightily in his generation and the generations after him have come to benefit from the ministry God gave him.

According to him, at the age 15, he was in the church but was not a born again Christian. In his book, I Believe in VISIONS, he states,

"I was born and raised Southern Baptist, but I had never been born again. You know, friends, you can be a church member and not be a Christian." (p.4)

I do perfectly agree with him. Many people call themselves Christians by virtue of belonging to a religious denomination. There are those who call themselves Christians because they attend church service occasionally.

However, the Bible does not say as many as are called Christians are the children of God, but as written in **Romans 8:14-16**

"[14] For as many as are led by the Spirit of God, these are sons of God. [15] For you did not receive the spirit of bondage again to fear, but you received the Spirit of adoption by whom we cry out, "Abba, Father." [16] The Spirit Himself bears witness with our spirit that we are children of God."

Does the Spirit of God bears witness with your spirit that you are a child of God?

For this reason, many will be cast out from the presence of God on the judgment day, even though, they were in the church, preached, cast out demons and healed the sick in the name of Jesus.

"[21] Not everyone who says to Me, 'Lord, Lord,' shall enter the kingdom of heaven, but he who does the will of My Father in heaven. [22] Many will say to Me in that day, 'Lord, Lord, have we not prophesied in Your name, cast out demons in Your name, and done many wonders in Your name?' [23] And then I will declare to them, 'I never knew you; depart from Me, you who practice lawlessness!'" (Matthew 7:21-23)

Even though, I have no doubt Kenneth E. Hagin was a man of God, I believe his visions of hell at the age of 15 was the work of the devil to terminate his life by tormenting his soul with those false pictures of hell. Yes. The devil has authority to kill those who belong to him; however, he has no power to take the life of a child of God. Although, God gave the devil power to touch Job, he was told not to take his life because job was a child of God.

"[6] And the LORD said to Satan, "Behold, he *is* in your hand, but spare his life."" (Job 2:6)

His description of hell as he narrated in his book, I Believe in VISIONS is not what hell really is.

In the book, he said,

"Earlier that evening before I was born again, my heart had stopped beating, and I died—my spirit left my body.

When my Spirit left my body, I went down, down, down until the lights of the earth faded way. I don't mean I fainted—I don't mean I was unconscious. I died. I have proof that I was actually dead. The Scriptures tell us about the lost being cast into outer darkness where there is weeping and gnashing of teeth (Matt. 25:30).

The farther down I went the blacker, the blacker it became until it was all blackness—I could not have seen my hand if it had been one inch in front of my eyes. And the farther down I went, the hotter and more stifling it became.

Finally below me, I could see lights flickering on the walls of the caverns of the damned. The lights were caused by the fires of hell. The giant, white-crested orb of flame pulled me, drawing me as a magnet draws metal to itself. I did not want to go into the jaws of hell, but just as metal jumps to the magnet, my unredeemed spirit was drawn to that place. I could not take my eyes off it. The intense heat beat me in the face. I came to the entrance of hell. Coming to the entrance of hell, I paused momentarily, because I did not want to go in. I sensed that one more foot, one more step, one more yard, and I would be gone forever and could not come out of that horrible place!

Upon reaching the bottom of the pit, I became conscious of some kind of spirit being by my side. I had not looked at him, because I could not take my gaze off of the fires of hell. But when I paused, that creature laid his hand on my arm to escort me in.

At the same moment, a Voice spoke from far above the blackness, above the earth, and above the heavens. I did not know if it was the voice of God, Jesus, and angel, or who it was. I did not see Him, and I do not know what He said, because He did not speak in English; He spoke in some other tongue. (Later I realised that was the Voice of God speaking from Heaven.)

When He spoke, His words reverberated throughout the region of the damned, shaking it like a leaf in the wind, and causing the creature to take his hand off my arm.

I did not turn around, but an unseen power, like a suction, pulled me up away from the fire, away from the intense heat, and back into the shadows of the absorbing darkness.

Then I began to ascend until I came to the top of the pit and saw the lights of the earth." (PP.4-11)

As at the time the prophet of God, Kenneth E. Hagin had this experience, he was not a child of God or not a born again Christian. He did not have any relationship with our Lord Jesus Christ. The devil, therefore, took advantage of that to torment him with those false visions of hell when he the devil realised he was at the point of death in order to send him out of this world before his appointed time. I believe Kenneth Hagin had a prophetic destiny to fulfil in this world, of which the devil was aware. He wanted to make sure that prophetic destiny was not fulfilled by cutting short his life at a point where he thought all hope was lost.

However, by the prayers of his mom, the Lord came to his rescue on the verge of death, when he, the devil was about taking his life. As our Lord came to the rescue of Moses when the devil disputed over his body, so he came to his rescue. The same way our Lord came to the rescue of all these people who have been tormented by the devil by these false visions of hell.

"9 Yet Michael the archangel, in contending with the devil, when he disputed about the body of Moses, dared not bring against him a reviling accusation, but said, "The Lord rebuke you!" (Jude 1:9)

Why did the devil dispute over the body of Moses?

The Bible tells us that when the children of Israel got to Kadesh on their way to the Promised Land, there was no water for them and consequently, began to complain against Moses and Aaron. Moses and Aaron turned to the Lord for help. The Lord gave him instruction on how to get the children of Israel water. However, out of anger, he disobeyed God. He was supposed to speak to the rock and not to strike the rock with the rod in his hand.

"[7] Then the LORD spoke to Moses, saying, [8] "Take the rod; you and your brother Aaron gather the congregation together. Speak to the rock before their eyes, and it will yield its water; thus you shall bring water for them out of the rock, and give drink to the congregation and their animals." [9] So Moses took the rod from before the LORD as He commanded him. [10] And Moses and Aaron gathered the assembly together before the rock; and he said to them, "Hear now, you rebels! Must we bring water for you out of this rock?" [11] Then Moses lifted his hand and struck the rock twice with his rod; and water came out abundantly, and the congregation and their animals drank." (Numbers 20:7-11)

The Lord, therefore, pronounced judgment on them because they did not honour Him in front of the congregation of Israel.

"[12] Then the LORD spoke to Moses and Aaron, "Because you did not believe Me, to hallow Me in the eyes of the children of Israel, therefore you shall not bring this assembly into the land which I have given them." (Numbers 20:12)

The devil knowing this disobedience by Moses and the judgment of God against Moses thought he was his and for that reason disputed over his body.

This is what happens when we disobey God and soil our relationship with Him. The devil makes claims on us as being his and torments us with various forms of afflictions to steal our joy, kill us before out appointed time and destroy our chances of having everlasting communion with our Lord Jesus Christ. Our Lord Jesus Christ said,

"[10] The thief does not come except to steal, and to kill, and to destroy. I have come that they may have life, and that they may have *it* more abundantly." (John 10:10)

This has always been the aim of the devil, to steal our joy by bring all kinds of pain on us, to take our lives and finally, lead us into everlasting destruction. However, our Lord has given us authority over him.

"[19]Behold, I give unto you power to tread on serpents and scorpions, and over all the power of the enemy: and nothing shall by any means hurt you." (Luke 10:19)

The man of God, Kenneth E. Hagin, unsaved by the time he had those visions, did not go to hell as he claimed he did, but was tormented by the devil by showing him false pictures of hell. Anyone who had had such an experience will believe he really went to hell, after all, the doctrine he came to meet said exactly what he saw in those visions of hell.

This does not mean he was not a man of God. It is just that the revelation of hell was not given to him. The Spirit of God, who knows the deep things of God, reveals to us things we need to know according to the will of God. If it has not been given to you, there is no way you will know.

"[12] Now we have received, not the spirit of the world, but the Spirit who is from God, that we might know the things that have been freely given to us by God." (1 Corinthians 2:12)

All of us believers came to inherit certain doctrines from our predecessors, which were later found to be false. Nevertheless, do these false doctrines make our predecessors non-believers? I do not think so, not at all. God in His own wisdom knows at what point in time He wants us, his children to come into knowledge of certain hidden truth. In fact, the Spirit of God reveals to us as He wills.

Chapter 8

THE LOVING AND MERCIFUL GOD

There is a sect of Christians that have argued that the loving and merciful nature of God will have been defeated if God will leave the souls of sinners in eternal condemnation. God is truly a loving and merciful God. God spoke through the prophet Hosea,

"[6]For I desire mercy and not sacrifice, And the knowledge of God more than burnt offerings." (Hosea 6:6)

God is indeed a merciful God that is the reason He did not listen to the plea of Jonah to destroy the people of Nineveh after he, Jonah had preached to them and they had repented.

"[1] But it displeased Jonah exceedingly, and he became angry. [2] So he prayed to the LORD, and said, "Ah, LORD, was not this what I said when I was still in my country? Therefore I fled previously to Tarshish; for I know that You *are* a gracious and merciful God, slow to

anger and abundant in loving-kindness, One who relents from doing harm."" (Jonah 4:1-3)

Therefore, it is not His wish that any should be found in hell, neither His desire that the wicked should perish.

"[23]Do I have any pleasure at all that the wicked should die?" says the Lord GOD, "*and* not that he should turn from his ways and live?" (Ezekiel 18:23)

"[32]For I have no pleasure in the death of one who dies," says the Lord GOD. "Therefore turn and live!" (Ezekiel 18:32)

"[11]'*As* I live,' says the Lord GOD, 'I have no pleasure in the death of the wicked, but that the wicked turn from his way and live. Turn, turn from your evil ways! For why should you die, O house of Israel?'" (Ezekiel 33:11)

That was the reason for sending His only begotten son to the earth to come and die for our sins, to make atonement for our sins and reconcile us to God.

"[16] For God so loved the world that He gave His only begotten Son, that whoever believes in Him should not perish but have everlasting life. [17] For God did not send His Son into the world to condemn the world, but that the world through Him might be saved." (John 3:16-17)

All you need to do is to accept Him as your Lord and Personal saviour.

"[9]That if you confess with your mouth the Lord Jesus and believe in your heart that God has raised Him from the dead, you will be saved. [10] For with the heart one believes unto righteousness, and with the mouth confession is made unto salvation. [13] For "whoever calls on the name of the LORD shall be saved."" (Romans 10:9-10, 13)

"[32] And it shall come to pass *That* whoever calls on the name of the LORD Shall be saved. For in Mount Zion and in Jerusalem there shall be deliverance, As the LORD has said, Among the remnant whom the LORD calls." (Joel 2:32)

"[17] And the Spirit and the bride say, "Come!" And let him who hears say, "Come!" And let him who thirsts come. Whoever desires, let him take the water of life freely." (Revelation 22:17)

After giving your life to Christ, you become a new creation of God.

"[17] Therefore, if anyone *is* in Christ, *he is* a new creation; old things have passed away; behold, all things have become new." (2 Corinthians 5:17)

Your old records in heaven will be wiped away by the blood of our Lord Jesus Christ and our Lord will not remember it any longer or will not hold it against you as stated in the scriptures;

"[21] "But if a wicked man turns from all his sins which he has committed, keeps all My statutes, and does what is lawful and right, he shall surely live; he shall not die. [22] None of the transgressions which he has committed shall be remembered against him; because of the righteousness which he has done, he shall live. [23] Do I have any pleasure at all that the wicked should die?" says the Lord GOD, "*and* not that he should turn from his ways and live?" (Ezekiel 18:21-23)

"[19] Repent therefore and be converted, that your sins may be blotted out, so that times of refreshing may come from the presence of the Lord," (Acts 3:19)

"[12] *For I will be merciful to their unrighteousness, and their sins and their lawless deeds I will remember no more."*" (Hebrews 8:12)

The decision to be in either hell or heaven has been left to us to make. God has left us to make our own choice.

"[15] SEE, I HAVE SET BEFORE YOU TODAY LIFE AND GOOD, DEATH AND EVIL, [16] in that I command you today to love the LORD your God, to walk in His ways, and to keep His commandments, His statutes, and His judgments, that you

may live and multiply; and the LORD your God will bless you in the land which you go to possess.[17] But if your heart turns away so that you do not hear, and are drawn away, and worship other gods and serve them, [18] I announce to you today that you shall surely perish; you shall not prolong *your* days in the land which you cross over the Jordan to go in and possess. [19] I CALL HEAVEN AND EARTH AS WITNESSES TODAY AGAINST YOU, *THAT* I HAVE SET BEFORE YOU LIFE AND DEATH, BLESSING AND CURSING; THEREFORE CHOOSE LIFE, THAT BOTH YOU AND YOUR DESCENDANTS MAY LIVE; [20] that you may love the LORD your God, that you may obey His voice, and that you may cling to Him, for He *is* your life and the length of your days; and that you may dwell in the land which the LORD swore to your fathers, to Abraham, Isaac, and Jacob, to give them." (Deuteronomy 30:15-20)

Even though the choice has been left to us to make, God is telling us to choose life instead of death.

A father knows what is best for his wards. The same way our Father in heaven knows what is good for us and He is telling us to choose life.

A loving and merciful God has made provision for us to be reconciled to Him after man fell in the Garden of Eden. He did this by sacrificing His only begotten son, the Lord Jesus Christ for the atonement of our sins.

"[8] But God demonstrates His own love toward us, in that while we were still sinners, Christ died for us." (Romans 5:8)

What manner of God is this? Even though we were separated from Him by our disobedience in the Garden of Eden, He still made provision for us to be reconciled to Him.

"[18] Now all things are of God, who has reconciled us to Himself through Jesus Christ, and has given us the ministry of reconciliation, [19] that is, that God was in Christ reconciling the world to Himself, not imputing their trespasses to them, and has committed to us the word of reconciliation." (2 Corinthians 5:18-19)

If after this provision to be reconciled to God and you still do not heed to the voice of God, do not forget, the same way He did not spare the devil and the fallen angels, the people in Noah's time, Sodom and Gomorrah, in the same way He will not spare the wicked on the judgment day.

"[41]Then He will also say to those on the left hand, 'Depart from Me, you cursed, into the everlasting fire prepared for the devil and his angels:" (Matthew 25:41)

Chapter 9

CHRIST IS THE WAY OF ESCAPE FROM GOD'S JUDGMENT

It has always been the plan of God to save you from hell.

"[11]For I know the thoughts that I think toward you, says the LORD, thoughts of peace and not of evil, to give you a future and a hope." (Jeremiah 29:11)

What is this plan of God?

It is in His plan to give you a future and hope.

It is in His plan to place you in a state where there will be no more sorrow or weeping.

"[4] And God will wipe away every tear from their eyes; there shall be no more death, nor sorrow, nor crying. There shall be no more pain, for the former things have passed away." (Revelation 21:4)

It is not His wish that the wicked should perish **(Ezekiel 18:23, 32)**. That was the reason He had to make Jonah, even though against his will, to go and preach to Nineveh for repentance so that they would escape His judgment.

"[1] Now the word of the LORD came to Jonah the second time, saying, [2] "Arise, go to Nineveh, that great city, and preach to it the message that I tell you." (Jonah 3:1)

The people of Nineveh repented at the preaching of Jonah and they were saved from the wrath of God, even though, Jonah was displeased by that.

"[1] But it displeased Jonah exceedingly, and he became angry. [2] So he prayed to the LORD, and said, "Ah, LORD, was not this what I said when I was still in my country? Therefore I fled previously to Tarshish; FOR I KNOW THAT YOU *ARE* A GRACIOUS AND MERCIFUL GOD, SLOW TO ANGER AND ABUNDANT IN LOVINGKINDNESS, ONE WHO RELENTS FROM DOING HARM. [3] Therefore now, O LORD, please take my life from me, for *it is* better for me to die than to live!" (Jonah 4:1-3)

Jonah was angry to the point of wishing death for himself. However, this is what the Lord says,

"[20] The soul who sins shall die. The son shall not bear the guilt of the father, nor the father

bear the guilt of the son. The righteousness of the righteous shall be upon himself, and the wickedness of the wicked shall be upon himself. [21] "But if a wicked man turns from all his sins which he has committed, keeps all My statutes, and does what is lawful and right, he shall surely live; he shall not die. [22] None of the transgressions which he has committed shall be remembered against him; because of the righteousness which he has done, he shall live. [23] Do I have any pleasure at all that the wicked should die?" says the Lord GOD, "*and* not that he should turn from his ways and live? [24] "But when a righteous man turns away from his righteousness and commits iniquity, and does according to all the abominations that the wicked *man* does, shall he live? All the righteousness which he has done shall not be remembered; because of the unfaithfulness of which he is guilty and the sin which he has committed, because of them he shall die.[25] "YET YOU SAY, 'THE WAY OF THE LORD IS NOT FAIR.' HEAR NOW, O HOUSE OF ISRAEL, IS IT NOT MY WAY WHICH IS FAIR, AND YOUR WAYS WHICH ARE NOT FAIR? [26] When a righteous *man* turns away from his righteousness, commits iniquity, and dies in it, it is because of the iniquity which he has done that he dies. [27] Again, when a wicked *man* turns away from the wickedness which he committed, and does what is lawful and right, he preserves himself alive. [28] Because he considers and turns away from all the

transgressions which he committed, he shall surely live; he shall not die. [29] YET THE HOUSE OF ISRAEL SAYS, 'THE WAY OF THE LORD IS NOT FAIR.' O HOUSE OF ISRAEL, IS IT NOT MY WAYS WHICH ARE FAIR, AND YOUR WAYS WHICH ARE NOT FAIR? [30] "Therefore I will judge you, O house of Israel, every one according to his ways," says the Lord GOD. "Repent, and turn from all your transgressions, so that iniquity will not be your ruin. [31] Cast away from you all the transgressions which you have committed, and get yourselves a new heart and a new spirit. For why should you die, O house of Israel? [32] For I have no pleasure in the death of one who dies," says the Lord GOD. "Therefore turn and live!"" (Ezekiel 18:20-32)

The above scripture shows that it is men, who wish the wicked to perish but not God. Jonah preferred a plant to live than men to live.

"[10] But the LORD said, "You have had pity on the plant for which you have not labored, nor made it grow, which came up in a night and perished in a night. [11] And should I not pity Nineveh, that great city, in which are more than one hundred and twenty thousand persons who cannot discern between their right hand and their left—and much livestock?"" (Jonah 4:10-11)

Should God not have mercy on His creation? The Bible tells we were created in the image and likeness of God.

"[26] Then God said, "LET US MAKE MAN IN OUR IMAGE, ACCORDING TO OUR LIKENESS; let them have dominion over the fish of the sea, over the birds of the air, and over the cattle, over all the earth and over every creeping thing that creeps on the earth." [27] SO GOD CREATED MAN IN HIS *OWN* IMAGE; IN THE IMAGE OF GOD HE CREATED HIM; MALE AND FEMALE HE CREATED THEM." (Genesis 1:26-27)

Should God destroy His image, even though, they have sinned against Him?

Should He not give us a chance to return to Him? Nineveh repented and returned to the Lord at the preaching of Jonah. The same way, God is using me to tell you there is always a chance for you to come back to Him so long as this age has not ended.

"[18]Come now, and let us reason together," Says the LORD, "Though your sins are like scarlet, They shall be as white as snow; Though they are red like crimson, They shall be as wool. (Isaiah 1:18)

Had Sodom and Gomorrah repented at the warnings of God, God's wrath would not have come upon them. God would have relented to His judgment upon them as He did to Nineveh. Nineveh was not destroyed because the whole nation repented at the preaching of Jonah, however, God could not find even 10 righteous men in Sodom and Gomorrah on the plea of Abraham to spare them of His judgment.

"[32]Then he said, "Let not the Lord be angry, and I will speak but once more: Suppose ten should be found there?" And He said, "I will not destroy *it* for the sake of ten."" (Genesis 18:32)

God sent His angels to Sodom and Gomorrah to verify whether the complaints against them were true. It is not to say that God did not know what was going on in Sodom and Gomorrah. He was aware for He is Omniscient, the all-knowing God.

"[20] And the LORD said, "Because the outcry against Sodom and Gomorrah is great, and because their sin is very grave, [21] I will go down now and see whether they have done altogether according to the outcry against it that has come to Me; and if not, I will know."" (Genesis 18:20-21)

The angels of God found out that the complaints against Sodom and Gomorrah were indeed true. After Lot had brought them into his house, given something to them to eat and were about to rest, the people of the town came around wanting to have carnal knowledge with the angels God had sent. Hence, God wiped them out from the surface of the earth.

"[4] Now before they lay down, the men of the city, the men of Sodom, both old and young, all the people from every quarter, surrounded the house. [5] And they called to Lot and said to him, "WHERE ARE THE MEN WHO CAME TO YOU TONIGHT? BRING THEM OUT TO US THAT WE MAY KNOW THEM *CARNALLY*." (Genesis 19:4-5)

One could reason out from the proceeding scripture that Lot had been preaching against their abominations, however, they did not listen to him. Jonah preached to Nineveh and they repented, nonetheless, Lot preached to the people of Sodom and Gomorrah, but they did not repent.

"[9] And they said, "Stand back!" Then they said, "THIS ONE CAME IN TO STAY *HERE*, AND HE KEEPS ACTING AS A JUDGE; now we will deal worse with you than with them . . ."" (Genesis 19:9)

As God sent His angels to go to Sodom and verify whether the complaints against them were true, the same way He sent His only begotten son to the earth to verify for Him whether the accusations of the devil against man was true. The son came to the earth and found out to be true that man fell in the Garden of Eden. This time around, God did not pass judgment on man but had mercy on man and made atonement for our sins by sacrificing

His only begotten son to end the accusation of the devil against man.

There is no longer excuse not to have the wrath of God coming on you if you do not repent and be saved from eternal destruction. Our Lord Jesus Christ came to die for our sins and paid the debt, which He did not owe on our behalves for all. All you need to do is to believe that He had made atonement for your sins and invite Him into your heart.

"[20] Behold, I stand at the door and knock. If anyone hears My voice and opens the door, I will come in to him and dine with him, and he with Me." (Revelation 3:20)

I wish to make it known to you that He is the only way to the Father. There is no other way.

He said, **"[6]I am the way, the truth, and the life. No one comes to the Father except through Me." (John 14:6)**

Chapter 10

CARRIERS OF THE MESSAGE STILL EXIST

"[27]Then he said, 'I beg you therefore, father, that you would send him to my father's house, [28] for I have five brothers, that he may testify to them, lest they also come to this place of torment.' [29] Abraham said to him, 'They have Moses and the prophets; let them hear them.' [30] And he said, 'No, father Abraham; but if one goes to them from the dead, they will repent.' [31] But he said to him, 'If they do not hear Moses and the prophets, neither will they be persuaded though one rise from the dead." (Vv.27-31)

God does not need to bring back Abraham, Isaac and Jacob, neither does He need to bring back Moses and the old prophets to warn you of hell and its torment.

He is using other vessels to do that for Him and he will continue to do that until the completion of this age. Many vessels are being recruited for the days are at hand and the fulfilment of every prophecy of God.

"[22] "Son of man, what *is* this proverb *that* you *people* have about the land of Israel, which says, 'The days are prolonged, and every vision fails'? [23] Tell them therefore, 'Thus says the Lord GOD: "I will lay this proverb to rest, and they shall no more use it as a proverb in Israel." But say to them, "The days are at hand, and the fulfilment of every vision. [24]For no more shall there be any false vision or flattering divination within the house of Israel. [25]For I *am* the LORD. I speak, and the word which I speak will come to pass; it will no more be postponed; for in your days, O rebellious house, I will say the word and perform it," says the Lord GOD.'" [26] Again the word of the LORD came to me, saying, [27] "Son of man, look, the house of Israel is saying, 'The vision that he sees *is* for many days *from now,* and he prophesies of times far off.' [28]Therefore say to them, 'Thus says the Lord GOD: "None of My words will be postponed any more, but the word which I speak will be done," says the Lord GOD.'"" (Ezekiel 12:22-28)

Many people have said," For they have been preaching of the second coming of the Lord Jesus Christ is at hand since 2000 years ago, but still He has not come. If their Lord Jesus Christ will indeed come, He will have come long time ago. We have been hearing this message that the end of the world is at hand since we were born but we have not seen anything."

Paul having a revelation of this warned us,

"[3] Knowing this first: that scoffers will come in the last days, walking according to their own lusts, [4] and saying, "Where is the promise of His coming? For since the fathers fell asleep, all things continue as *they were* from the beginning of creation." (2 Peter 3:3-4)

However, this is what the Lord is saying, "The time has come when I will put all these saying to rest. I will bring an end to this and none of My words will be postponed any longer."

"[22] And unless those days were shortened, no flesh would be saved; but for the elect's sake those days will be shortened." (Matthew 24:22)

"[8] But, beloved, do not forget this one thing, that with the Lord one day *is* as a thousand years, and a thousand years as one day. [9] The Lord is not slack concerning *His* promise, as some count slackness, but is longsuffering toward us, not willing that any should perish but that all should come to repentance." (2 Peter 3:8-9)

[7]"Behold, I am coming quickly! Blessed *is* he who keeps the words of the prophecy of this book." (Revelation 22:7)

He is no longer going to delay in His coming.

"[24] The LORD of hosts has sworn, saying, "Surely, as I have thought, so it shall come to pass, And as I have purposed, *so* it shall stand: "(Isaiah 14:24)

Do not be despaired, neither give up on the faith, remembering what the Apostle Paul said,

"[8] *We are* hard-pressed on every side, yet not crushed; *we are* perplexed, but not in despair; [9] persecuted, but not forsaken; struck down, but not destroyed—" (2 Corinthians 4:8-9)

Nor let your love for God grow cold as the Bible says,

"[12] And because lawlessness will abound, the love of many will grow cold. [13] But he who endures to the end shall be saved." (Matthew 24:12-13)

The Lord Jesus Christ again warns us in Revelation.

"[4] Nevertheless I have *this* against you, that you have left your first love. [5] Remember therefore from where you have fallen; repent and do the first works, or else I will come to

you quickly and remove your lampstand from its place—unless you repent." (Revelation 2:4-5)

Now let us go back to our main scripture, Mark 16:

"[27]Then he said, 'I beg you therefore, father, that you would send him to my father's house, [28] for I have five brothers, that he may testify to them, lest they also come to this place of torment.' (Vv.27-28)

The Richman, ignorant of the fact that God has many servants of His still preaching the message of salvation, thought Lazarus was the only one who could do that and hence wanted him to go back to earth to preach to his brothers.

"[29] Abraham said to him, 'They have Moses and the prophets; let them hear them." (v.29)

Yes. God is using new vessels to warn you of hell. He has put His word in new vessels to be declared to you for you to know the truth about hell and hell fire.

"28 And it shall come to pass afterward That I will pour out My Spirit on all flesh; Your sons and your daughters shall prophesy, Your old men shall dream dreams, Your young men shall see visions.[29]And also on *My* menservants and on *My* maidservants I will pour out My Spirit in those days." (Joel 2:28-30)

"30 And he said, 'No, father Abraham; but if one goes to them from the dead, they will repent.' 31 But he said to him, 'If they do not hear Moses and the prophets, neither will they be persuaded though one rise from the dead." (Vv.30-31)

Abraham was right in saying so. Yes, even though, One, our Lord Jesus Christ, who had preached several times in the scriptures about hell, rose from the dead, people still do not believe there is hell.

The Lord Jesus Christ said, **"18 I *am* He who lives, and was dead, and behold, I am alive forevermore. Amen. And I have the keys of Hades and of Death." (Revelation 1:18)**

What can I say more?

Hell is not a state that any soul should ever be. It was prepared for the Devil and the demons and not for you.

"41Then He will also say to those on the left hand, 'Depart from Me, you cursed, into the everlasting fire prepared for the devil and his angels:" (Matthew 25:41)

However, the decision for you to be there lies in your hand. God has given you the free will to make your choice.

Chapter 11

IS YOUR NAME WRITTEN IN HEAVEN?

Our Lord Jesus Christ giving the parable of the rich man and Lazarus made mention of the names of Lazarus and Abraham but not the rich man's.

"[19] "There was a certain rich man who was clothed in purple and fine linen and fared sumptuously every day. [20] But there was a certain beggar named Lazarus, full of sores, who was laid at his gate, . . . [22] So it was that the beggar died, and was carried by the angels to Abraham's bosom. The rich man also died and was buried." (Luke 16:19-20, 22)

Why did our Lord Jesus Christ make mention the names of Lazarus and Abraham, but not that of the rich man?

Our Lord Jesus Christ said,

"[21] Not everyone who says to Me, 'Lord, Lord,' shall enter the kingdom of heaven, but he

who does the will of My Father in heaven. [22] Many will say to Me in that day, 'Lord, Lord, have we not prophesied in Your name, cast out demons in Your name, and done many wonders in Your name?' [23] AND THEN I WILL DECLARE TO THEM, 'I NEVER KNEW YOU; DEPART FROM ME, YOU WHO PRACTICE LAWLESSNESS!'" (Matthew 7:21-23)

He did not mention the name of the rich man because He never knew him. This is because his name was not in the Book of Life. However, He knew Abraham and Lazarus because their names were found in the Book of life. This is exactly what will happen on the judgment day. Our Lord Jesus Christ will declare to all those who practised lawlessness that He never knew them because He could not find their names in the Book of Life.

The ultimate goal of every believer is to be in heaven. Nonetheless, you cannot be in heaven without your name written in the Book of Life. You cannot enter the new city of Jerusalem without your name in the Book of Life.

"[27] But there shall by no means enter it anything that defiles, or causes an abomination or a lie, but only those who are written in the Lamb's Book of Life." (Revelation 21:27)

When the seventy disciples our Lord Jesus Christ sent came back rejoicing for the demons were subject to them at the mention of the name Jesus, our Lord Jesus told them not to rejoice because the demons were subject to them but rejoice for their names were recorded in heaven.

"[20]Nevertheless do not rejoice in this, that the spirits are subject to you, but rather rejoice because your names are written in heaven." (Luke 10:20)

Three times has the Lord open my eyes to see my name in the Book of Life and this was when I began to evangelise. I am not implying only those who evangelise have their names written in the Book of Life. I believe God showed me that just to affirm what has been written in the scriptures.

In fact, you do not need your eyes to be opened to see your name in the Book of life before you believe your name has been written in the Book of Life. So long as you are a child of God, have in mind that your name is in the Book of Life.

The Bible does not tell us Apostle Paul saw the names of the people he worked with in the Book of Life. I think he believed as his name was in the Book of Life, so those he worked with for the sake of the gospel of Christ had their names in the Book of Life as well. This was the reason he said,

"[3] And I urge you also, true companion, help these women who labored with me in the gospel, with Clement also, and the rest of my fellow workers, WHOSE NAMES *ARE* IN THE BOOK OF LIFE." (Philippians 4:3)

The Book of Life contains the names of the children of God. One may therefore ask, "How do I know that I am a child of God?" You can only know through the Spirit of God.

"[14] For as many as are led by the Spirit of God, these are sons of God. [15] For you did not receive the spirit of bondage again to fear, but you received the Spirit of adoption by whom we cry out, "Abba, Father." [16] The Spirit Himself bears witness with our spirit that we are children of God." (Romans 8:14-16)

Therefore, as long as you remain a child of God, believe that your name is in the Book of Life. Your name will only be wiped out when you cease to be a child of God.

The Bible tells us that while Moses was on the mountain with God for forty days and forty nights and God was giving him the Ten Commandments, the children of Israel made for them a gold calf, which they began to worship. The anger of the Lord rose against them for worshipping a creature rather than the Creator. Moses pleaded with God preferring his name was scrap from the Book of Life to the Lord wiping out the perpetrators.

However, the Lord told him He would rather blot out the names of those who sinned against Him.

"[31] Then Moses returned to the LORD and said, "Oh, these people have committed a great sin, and have made for themselves a god of gold! [32] Yet now, if You will forgive their sin—but if not, I PRAY, BLOT ME OUT OF YOUR BOOK WHICH YOU HAVE WRITTEN." [33] And the LORD said to Moses, "WHOEVER HAS SINNED AGAINST ME, I WILL BLOT HIM OUT OF MY BOOK."" (Exodus 32:31-33)

Do not be deceived into thinking that after accepting our Lord Jesus Christ as your Lord and Saviour and you go back to your old way of doing things, Jehovah will still see you as His child. Have it in mind that there is no way the unrighteous will be counted with the righteous.

"[28] Let them be blotted out of the book of the living, And not be written with the righteous." (Psalm 69:28)

God's children will be delivered from the wrath of God that will come upon the children of perdition.

"[1] "At that time Michael shall stand up, The great prince who stands *watch* over the sons

of your people; And there shall be a time of trouble, Such as never was since there was a nation, *Even* to that time. And at that time your people shall be delivered, Every one who is found written in the book." (Daniel 12:1)

Our Lord Jesus Christ promises us of keeping our names in The Book of Life if we hold fast to the faith until the end.

"[5] He who overcomes shall be clothed in white garments, and I will not blot out his name from the Book of Life; but I will confess his name before My Father and before His angels." (Revelation 3:5)

My prayer is that you will keep up to the faith so that your name is not wiped out from the Book of Life. According to the revelation of our Lord Jesus Christ to John, those whose names were not found in the Book of Life were cast into the lake of fire **(Revelation 20:15)**.

Chapter 12

CONCLUSION

Hell is a state of doom and eternal separation from God. It is a thirst for the Word of God, which can never be quenched. A state an unrighteous soul ends up when he is cut-off from the presence of God. Accept our Lord Jesus Christ today and escape hell and its torments. Nothing can save you from the wrath of God except our Lord Jesus Christ.

"[12] Nor is there salvation in any other, for there is no other name under heaven given among men by which we must be saved." (Acts 4:12)

All you need to do is to confess your sins to Him.

"[9] If we confess our sins, He is faithful and just to forgive us *our* sins and to cleanse us from all unrighteousness." (1 John 1:9)

"[9]That if you confess with your mouth the Lord Jesus and believe in your heart that God has raised Him from the dead, you will be

saved. [10] For with the heart one believes unto righteousness, and with the mouth confession is made unto salvation. [11] For the Scripture says, "*Whoever believes on Him will not be put to shame.*" [12] For there is no distinction between Jew and Greek, for the same Lord over all is rich to all who call upon Him. [13] For "*whoever calls on the name of the LORD shall be saved.*" (Romans 10:9-13)

In case you wish to accept our Lord Jesus Christ as your Lord and Saviour, just say these words.

Dear Lord Jesus Christ,

I know I am a sinner. I have come to know the truth today that you came to die for my sins. I surrender my life to you and I accept you as my Lord and Saviour. Please forgive me my sins as your word says if I confess my sins to you, you are just and faithful to forgive me my sins and cleanse me from all unrighteousness.

I thank you Lord for forgiveness of my sins. Amen.

I will end with this song by Gary Sadler;

Lord I thirst for You.

CHORUS:

Lord, I thirst for You

I long to be in Your presence

My soul will wait on You

Father, draw me nearer

Draw me nearer

To the beauty of Your holiness

VERSE:

I will wait for You, Almighty God

In the beauty of Your holiness

I will worship You, Almighty God

In the beauty of Your holiness

Retrieved from (http://www.topchristianlyrics.com/2009/11/09/lord-i-thirst-for-you-lyrics-gary-sadler/)

Graham, B. (1993, November 15). Of angels, devils and messages from God. *Time Magazine*. Retrieved July 10, 2011 from (http://www.time.com/time/magazine/article/0,9171,979587,00.html#ixzz1RjeE0m4h)

Graham, B. (2010).Storm Warning. Tennessee: Thomas Nelson.

Hagin, K. E. (1984).I Believe in VISIONS. Oklahoma:Faith Library Publications.

Paul II, J. (1999). General Audience. Retrieved July 10, 2011 from http://www.vatican.va/holy_father/john_paul_ii/audiences/1999/documents/hf_jp-ii_aud_28071999_en.html.

Sadler, G. (1992 Integrity's Hosanna! Music). Lord I thirst for you. Retrieved from (http://www.topchristianlyrics.com/2009/11/09/lord-i-thirst-for-you-lyrics-gary-sadler/)

Wiese, B. (1998). 23 Minutes in Hell. Retrieved July 23, 2011 from http://spiritlessons.com/documents/billwiese_23minutesinhell_text.htm.

Wright, N.T. (2008). Where Is Hell Located? Retrieved July 10, 2011 from http://www.100huntley.com/video.php?id=8Zk31Uc_pCY.